By Laura Williams
Translated By Akosua Boateng

da

to sleep

dware

to take a bath

wea

to crawl

di agorɔ

to play

tenase

to sit

su

to cry

gyina

to stand

bɔ wonsam

to clap

kenkan

to read

didi

to eat

nom

to drink

sere

to laugh

fam

to hug

nante

to walk

dwane

to run

fe ano

to kiss

huri

to jump

nwunwu

to tickle

sa
to dance

noa

to cook

bu nkotodwe

to kneel

pia

to push

twe

to pull

twerɛ

to write

to dwom

to sing

In the same collection

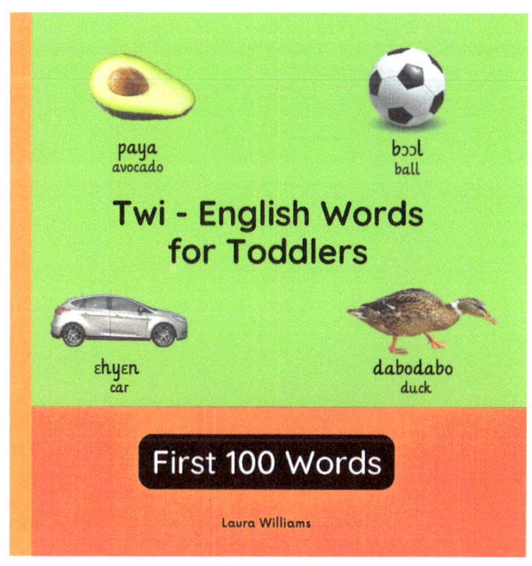

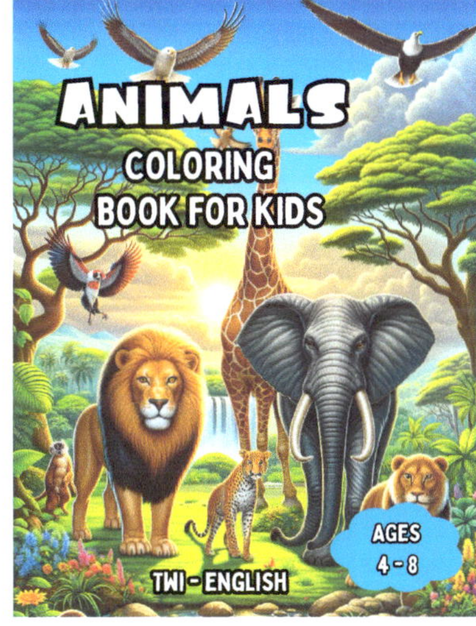

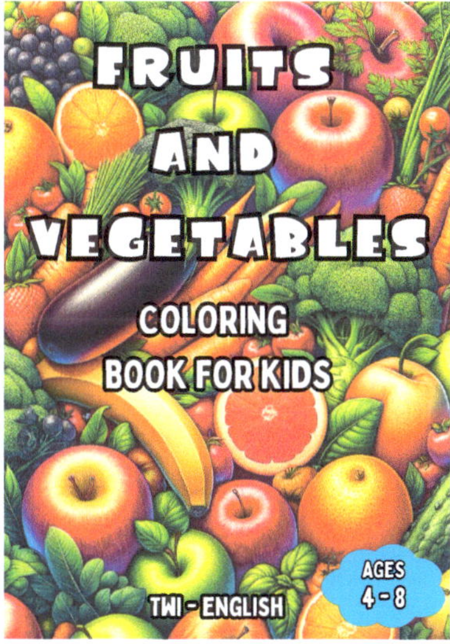